The World of Work
Choosing a Career in the Helping Professions

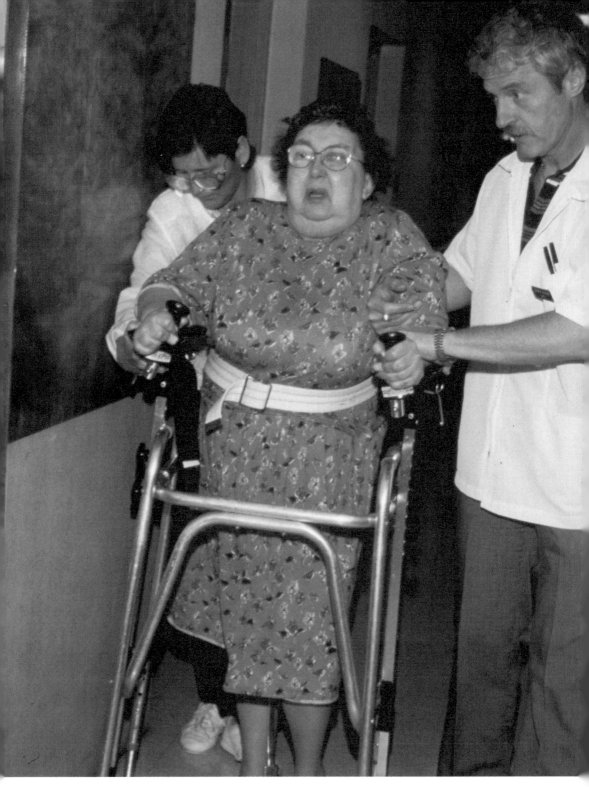

If you enjoy helping other people, you may want to consider a career in the helping professions.

The World of Work
Choosing a Career in the Helping Professions

Pat Tretout

THE ROSEN PUBLISHING GROUP, INC.
NEW YORK

Published in 1997 by The Rosen Publishing Group, Inc.
29 East 21st Street, New York, NY 10010

Copyright © 1997 by The Rosen Publishing Group, Inc.
First Edition

All rights reserved. No part of this book may be reproduced in any form without permission in writing from the publisher, except by a reviewer.

Manufactured in the United States of America.

Library of Congress Cataloging-in-Publication Data

Tretout, Pat.
    Choosing a career in the helping professions / Pat Tretout.
      p. cm. — (The world of work)
    Includes bibliographical references and index.
    Summary: Introduces various careers that involve helping people with problems, including jobs in health care, human services, and relief organizations.
    ISBN 0-8239-2272-3
    1. Human services—Vocational guidance—United States—Juvenile literature. 2. Social service—Vocational guidance—United States—Juvenile literature. 3. Medical care—Vocational guidance—United States—Juvenile literature. [1. Human services—Vocational guidance. 2. Social service—Vocational guidance. 3. Medical care—Vocational guidance. 4. Vocational guidance.]
I. Title. II. Series.
HV10.5.T74   1996
361'.0023'73—dc20   96-26407
                                                                             CIP
                                                                              AC

Contents

Introduction	7
1. What Are the Helping Professions?	9
2. Health Care: Helping the Sick	14
3. Human Services: Helping People in Your Community	27
4. National Service: Helping People in Your Country	35
5. International Jobs: Helping People in the World	43
6. Finding the Right Job for You	52
Glossary	59
For More Information	60
For Further Reading	62
Index	63

A career in the helping professions can be rewarding and satisfying.

Introduction

The writer Mark Twain once said that the "luckiest people in the world get to do all year long what they like to do on their summer vacation."

Having a job means more than getting a paycheck. Look around you. You will see people working in a variety of jobs. The luckiest and happiest people are those who enjoy their jobs. The first step is knowing what you like to do and what you're good at.

Have you ever helped a blind person cross a busy street? You may remember how good it felt to help someone. Have you ever listened to a friend's heartache? Then you know how important it is to be caring. If you can understand how other people feel, listen patiently to problems, and like to be involved in projects helping other people, you may want to consider a career in the helping professions.

Health care is just one area of the helping professions.

What Are the Helping Professions?

1

Generally speaking, the *helping professions* are jobs that help people with problems. This book will explain four broad categories of helping professions:

- *health care*—the tending of the sick
- *human services*—providing support in a particular community
- *national service*—helping people on a national level
- *international service*—helping people on an international level

You can decide where you would like to work, with whom you would like to work, and how you would like to help.

The Ladder of Opportunity
In each of the categories of helping professions, there are many different types of jobs, work environments, and salaries. This

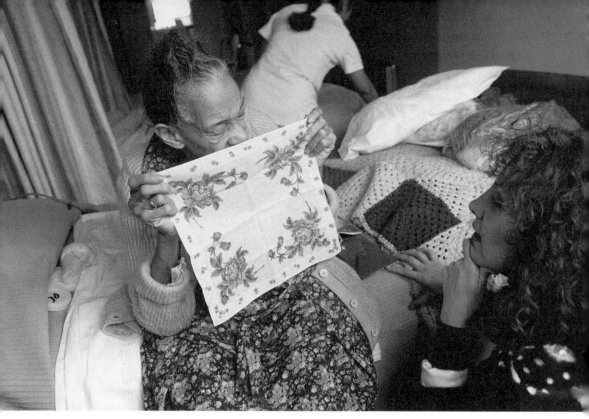

As a volunteer, you have the chance to learn about a job by actually doing it.

book will trace the ladder of opportunity in each area of the helping professions.

Each of these areas has several stages in the field: volunteer, entry-level, paraprofessional, and professional. Each step requires training, experience, and improvement of skills.

Step One: Volunteer

A *volunteer* position is one for which you are not paid. Volunteering is a kind of informal training.

You can also do an internship or an apprenticeship when you are in school. An *intern* is an advanced student or recent graduate who gains supervised practical experience. An *apprentice* learns a job under the direction of a skilled worker. Interns and apprentices may be paid or not. As an intern or apprentice, you "learn the ropes" and find out what the job is all about. You can watch the people who work in the profession and decide if you would like to be part of it.

As a volunteer, intern, or apprentice, you are likely to learn of job openings before they become known publicly. You may have a chance to apply for the job before others. You also have the benefit of knowing people in the profession beforehand.

Finally, volunteering is a wonderful opportunity for networking. *Networking* is the process of getting to know people in your field and establishing contacts for the future. Networking never stops. Your contacts form a web of support and knowledge. You should establish a system to file people's names and positions. Stay in touch with these people to exchange professional information. Keep up with moves in their careers.

Step Two: Entry-Level

In the helping professions, the *entry-level* position is usually that of aide or assistant. An *aide* or *assistant* helps the next level of worker,

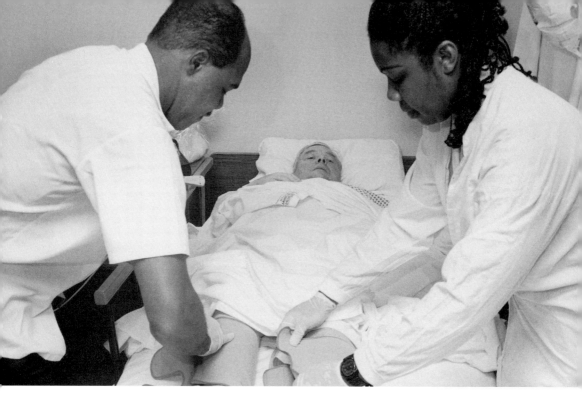
A paraprofessional is a trained assistant.

the paraprofessional, with his or her daily work load. The job of aide can be full-time or part-time. Aides receive either an hourly wage or a yearly salary. Such positions usually require a high school diploma or a certificate saying you've passed the general educational development, or GED, tests.

Step Three: Paraprofessional

A *paraprofessional* is a full-time employee who assists professionals in a given profession. The requirements are usually an associate's degree from a community college and state certification. To gain state certification, you must take a course in your field and pass a test. For example, nurse's aides must be state certified to work with mentally disabled patients. Most employers also prefer hands-on experience. The title of a job at this level is often referred to as *associate*.

Step Four: Professional

A *professional* is at the head of his or her field. The position usually requires a bachelor's or master's degree as well as state certification. The course of study usually takes several years and is quite intensive.

The first step of the ladder is at your feet. It's up to you how far you wish to climb.

Questions to Ask Yourself

The helping professions cover a wide variety of careers. It can be tough to narrow them down. Think about these questions as you read about some of your choices. 1) Are you a good listener, or are you more action-oriented? 2) Would you like to work close to home or would you rather go overseas? Why? 3) Is there a specific group of people that you would enjoy working with? Why?

Health Care: Helping the Sick 2

This chapter focuses on *health-care workers*. They help with people's physical needs.

Candy Stripers

A *candy striper* works in a hospital or medical facility. They are called candy stripers because of their pink aprons. Candy stripers can work on either a volunteer or paid basis. Candy stripers help sick people feel more comfortable in hospitals. Their duties include delivering newspapers, flowers, and mail to patients. Most candy stripers are students. They come to work after classes. Many elderly people also work as candy stripers.

Kathy, Nurse's Aide

Kathy works as a nurse's aide in a personal care facility outside of Philadephia, Pennsylvania. There she met Stanley, who changed her life. Stanley is a forgetful seventy-eight-year-old. Kathy has to remind

Nurse's aides may develop close relationships with the people under their care.

him to get up at mealtime, and to prepare for shower night on Tuesdays and Thursdays. Kathy spends many hours working with Stanley. They have become good friends. Kathy has a new understanding of and respect for elderly people. She feels good about herself when she helps others.

Nurse's Aides

Nurse's aides work in personal care facilities and in nursing homes. *Personal care facilities* are places where elderly people or people with special needs live. The residents there can take care of themselves for the most part. Nurse's aides help residents by giving them cues. Cues are reminders, such as when to eat meals, take showers, and wake up.

In *nursing homes*, the elderly residents are often physically disabled and need medical care. For these jobs, nurse's aides must be state certified. Salaries range between $17,000 and $22,000 a year.

To receive state certification, the student must complete a 92- to 120-hour course. The requirements vary by state. To find out more about state certification in your home state, contact your local branch of the American Red Cross. At the end of the course, the nurse's aide must pass both a written exam and a practical exam. The practical exam consists of a series of tasks, such as taking a patient's temperature and blood pressure, removing and cleaning dentures, and proper hand washing.

Physical Therapists

Physical therapists help people regain physical mobility after an accident, illness, or surgery. A physical therapist works closely with a patient's doctor to relieve pain and increase the mobility of the affected body part. To be a physical therapist you will need a master's degree in physical therapy. Then you must be certified by the state. Salaries vary according to location, but generally start between $35,000 and $50,000 a year. Physical therapy is a rapidly growing field.

A *physical therapist's assistant* helps the therapist as needed. The assistant often teaches patients how to use crutches, a wheelchair, or other tools. Assistants also keep records of cases and handle much of the paperwork. To become an assistant, you must earn a bachelor's degree and become state certified. Salaries at the assistant level range from $26,000 to $43,000 per year.

A physical therapist's assistant is a paraprofessional. She may help teach a patient how to use a machine or do an exercise.

A *physical therapist's aide* may help with paperwork, taking histories of patients, as well as other tasks. Aides must have a high school diploma or certificate showing you've passed the GED tests. Salaries can start as high as $18,000.

Emergency Medical Services

When you hear a siren or see an ambulance racing down the street toward the hospital, it's probably a paramedic or an *emergency medical technician*, or EMT, in action. These are the people who come when you dial 911 for emergency assistance anywhere in the United States. Their jobs fall under the broad wing of the *Emergency Medical Services*, which also include police officers and firefighters.

When someone is injured, either in an accident, during a violent crime, or by some other method, EMTs and paramedics transport the person to a hospital, maintaining the victim's condition while in transit.

Jeff, Lifeguard and EMT

Jeff works as a lifeguard. He is also trained as an emergency medical technician. Last Wednesday morning, his beeper went off before he reported for work. The dispatcher said, "Cardiac arrest in progress. Get to the scene!" Jeff caught his breath. Someone was having a heart attack.

Jeff headed for the site in an ambulance. When he arrived, two police officers and an off-duty firefighter were already doing CPR. But he was the first CPT, or cardiopulmonary technician, to arrive with the ambulance. That meant that he was the senior person on the scene; he was in charge.

The man's heart was not beating. He was not breathing. Jeff helped the emergency medical team hook the man up to the defibrillator, a machine that sends a shock to the chest. By then the paramedic had arrived. Now the paramedic took charge. He was the highest person on the team. A paramedic can apply lifesaving drugs to the patient.

The team moved the patient into the ambulance, and the paramedic administered the drugs. Right before their eyes, the patient recovered. Everyone breathed a sigh of relief.

Dedicated people like Jeff can mean the difference between life and death. EMTs and paramedics are professionals who know their jobs well, can think on their feet, and are cool under pressure. These jobs are often stressful, but they are also highly rewarding. They require relatively modest training, but they offer one of the highest levels of job satisfaction in the helping professions. But what are the differences between an EMT and a paramedic?

Emergency Medical Technicians

The emergency medical technician, or EMT, is the first level of trained life support a patient is likely to meet following a car accident or an emergency health situation. EMTs are certified to take blood pressure, perform cardiopulmonary resuscitation, or CPR, and the Heimlich maneuver, which removes an

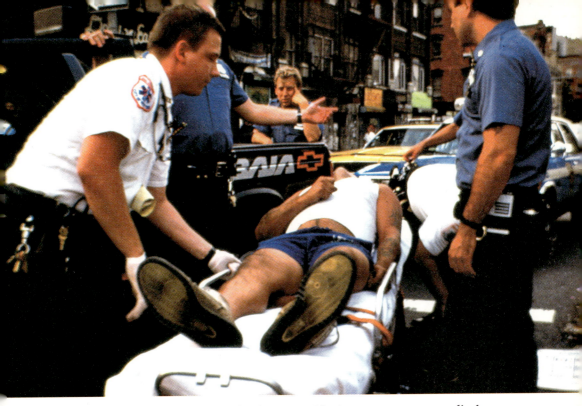

EMTS are trained to help people after an accident or an emergency medical situation.

obstacle from a person's windpipe. They can also give oxygen. Most community colleges offer the minimum requirement of 120 hours of study along with the proper certification. The salary range is from $18,000 to $25,000, depending on the state you live in. As you accumulate experience, training, and credits, your skills are reevaluated, and your salary can increase. With enough further training, you can become a paramedic.

Paramedics

Paramedics do work similar to that of EMTS, but they are state certified to practice more advanced procedures and have more responsibilities. They can administer specific drugs and intravenous, or IV, solutions. Paramedics report for duty at hospitals. From there they are sent to emergency sites, often along with an EMT, who is second-in-command.

To become a paramedic, you must first become an EMT. Then you continue your schooling for another eighteen months or two years. Starting salaries for paramedics range between $25,000 and $27,000 a year.

Home Health Care

Home health care offers long-term or short-term assistance to people who are recovering from an illness or surgery, or who are terminally ill. A person who is terminally ill won't recover from the illness he or she has. The basic tasks of a *home health care provider* are light housework, grocery shopping, and cooking. Home health care covers the physical needs of a patient, and the quality of his or her life.

These services, such as homemaker services, meal services, and shopping services, are frequently used by the elderly, homebound, or bedridden. A home health care aide helps a person bathe and dress, prepares food,

Home health care is a growing industry because the number of elderly people is increasing.

and takes him or her out for fresh air.

A home health care agency assigns a home health care person to work between four and eight hours a day, from one to five days a week, depending on the needs of the patient. Home health care workers earn minimum wage, and there are no formal educational requirements. This position is rewarding because the presence of a home health care worker is often critical to a patient's physical well-being.

There are more than 8,000 home health care agencies in the United States. Look in the yellow pages of your phone book for agencies or the classified section of your local newspaper for job listings.

Medical Assistants

Medical assistants work under the direction of a doctor to assist in the examination and treatment of patients. They interview patients, measure vital signs, such as pulse rate, temperature, blood pressure, weight, and height, and record information on patients' charts. They also prepare treatment rooms for examination of patients by draping patients with a covering, and positioning instruments and equipment. During the examination, medical assistants hand instruments and materials to a doctor as directed. After the examination, they clean and sterilize instruments. They take inventories and order medical supplies. They operate equipment for X rays, electrocardiographs, and other routine tests. They give injections, perform routine laboratory tests, schedule appointments, and receive money for bills.

Physicians

To become a *physician*, or medical doctor, you must complete a long course of training. Before applying for medical school, a student must first have a bachelor's degree from a four-year college. Then a student must attend medical school, which takes four years to

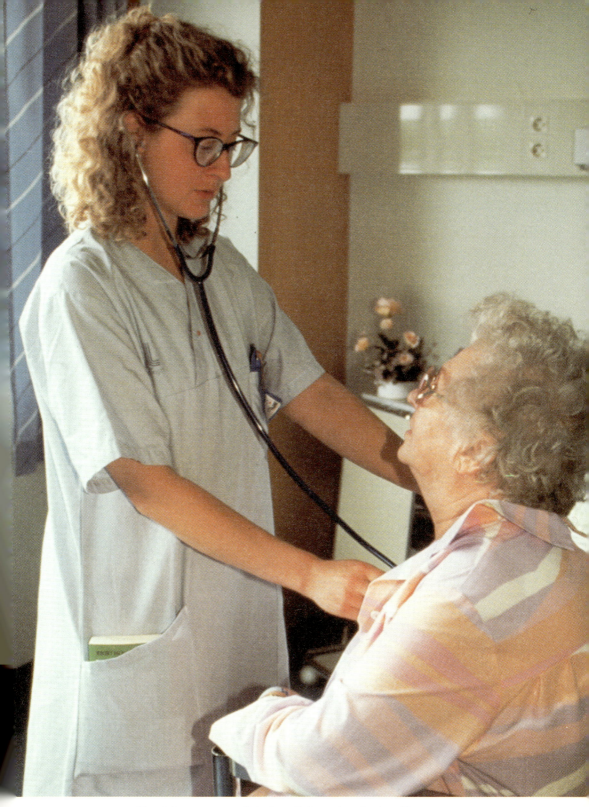
Physicians may work in hospitals or in private offices.

complete. Next the doctor must complete an internship and a residency at a hospital. These are the doctor's first jobs, when he or she works in a hospital learning from experienced doctors. These generally take another four years. After several more years of practice and training, doctors are eligible to take the board certification exams. Doctors can work in hospitals, private practice, medical groups, relief organizations, or government agencies.

Questions to Ask Yourself

Many career choices involve caring for people's physical well-being. 1) Which area, if any, appeals to you: therapy, emergency medical services, or medicine? 2) Are you comfortable around the sight of blood? Or would you rather provide administrative support? 3) Are you comfortable dealing with the public, or would you prefer to work in an office? 4) How long are you willing to spend in school?

Human Services: Helping People in Your Community

3

While health-care workers treat a person's physical needs, human services workers treat a person's emotional needs. For example, *social workers*, one kind of human services worker, look at a person's relationships. They examine a client's family interactions and environment. Social workers try to create support networks for people. They help abused, neglected, homeless, and depressed people. Through counseling, human services workers try to help people become active, productive members of society. *Counseling* means giving advice.

Compared to some other professions, human services work does not pay very well. However, on a personal level, it can be very rewarding. Human services work brings you into contact with people every day. To be good at this kind of work, you need to like people. The challenge of the work is to help people become independent, and not to rely on the services that you provide. A person under the guidance of a good human services worker learns how to help himself.

Human services workers need to be good listeners. They have to be good role models for their clients. To gain the trust of their clients, they must be able to keep secrets. Human services workers also must be resourceful. They have to find creative solutions to difficult problems.

Counseling

A *counselor* encourages a client to think about his or her problems and proposes ways to deal with the problems. It is up to the client to decide how to handle the next step. The counselor then may help the client put the plan into action.

To enjoy the field of counseling, you need patience, compassion, and a strong desire to help others. You also need good communication skills and a sense of responsibility.

There are three types of counseling:

Case work is working with individual clients. A *case aide* may perform such duties as driving clients to dining halls for meals.

Group work calls for working with several clients at a time. This is usually done in a setting such as a hospital or halfway house. In a halfway house, a group of people make the transition from a prison or an alcohol or drug rehabilitation center back to the community at large.

Community organization work is done by a counselor in coordination with several other agencies. This service is aimed at helping an entire community solve a problem, such as how to help the homeless in their area.

Kate, Social Worker

Kate works in a community health van in New York City. The services that the van provides are free. The clients include homeless people and alcoholics. When she was choosing a career, Kate decided that she did not want to work at a bank or in a store. She did not want a nine-to-five office job. Instead, Kate decided that she wanted hands-on work in her community. She wanted to work directly with people, helping them to solve their problems.

"I have learned more from the homeless people in New York City than I ever did in school. I really feel like I am providing a valuable service in my community."

Social Workers

Social workers are often the first people met by a person in need of human services. Social workers spend part of their day in an office setting or group residence and the rest of it going to people's homes.

Child welfare workers help children and teens in abusive situations. They investigate and report instances of neglect or abuse and take legal action if necessary to place children in foster homes.

Medical social workers help patients and their families when diseases such as AIDS or Alzheimer's cause suffering. They help a patient and his family adjust to the new situation.

School social workers work within school systems to help children who have emotional problems. These students are often put into special education classrooms simply because they can't control their behavior. A school social worker works with the family of such a student to try to integrate him or her back into the general school population. Social workers also teach classroom teachers how to deal with problem students.

Industrial or *occupational social workers* work within a personnel department of a

There are many types of social work, including child welfare.

business to help employees cope with job pressures or personal problems that affect the quality of their work.

Gerontology social workers run support groups for the elderly. They also advise the elderly and their family members on the subjects of long-term housing and health care.

A bachelor's degree, and often a master's degree, is the minimum requirement for a professional position in social work. However, small agencies may accept some community college courses in psychology or sociology. In such places, you may find a position available as a record keeper or an aide to one of the social workers on the staff. Salaries usually start at $18,000.

Other Human Services Careers

Counselors and their assistants work with individuals or groups needing a broad range of mental health services. For example, *child abuse counselors* and their assistants work to save children from abuse and neglect. *Gerontology counselors* and aides work with the elderly in nursing homes, hospitals, and retirement communities. *Alcohol and drug abuse counselors* and their assistants work in hospitals or halfway houses or in private practice. *Community outreach workers* help former prisoners re-enter society as law-abiding citizens.

Vocational rehabilitation counselors and their assistants help people with physical disabilities or mental impairments find jobs. These counselors develop job openings within the community for their clients. They also work with drug or alcohol addicts or family members affected by addicts. They help parolees adjust to life outside prison. These counselors help clients structure their time, manage their money, and set realistic goals for themselves.

The tasks of an assistant for any of the above counseling careers are many. They may include helping a client get benefits such as health or life insurance; examining tax returns to see if the client is eligible for federal aid such as welfare or food stamps; or arranging transportation for a patient to get to group meetings, adult day care programs, or doctor's appointments. In addition, an assistant provides a client with emotional support and makes sure that the client is receiving all the services he or she is entitled to.

Many community colleges offer a one-year certificate program or a two-year associate's program in human services. Though it takes a lot of effort, helping people to overcome their disabilities and to win back their independence is a most satisfying task.

Mary, Volunteer

Mary works as a volunteer on the children's psychiatric floor at her local hospital. She always knew that she wanted to work with children, but she didn't know how rewarding the work was going to be until she met Tommy.

Tommy was only four years old when he arrived at Mary's unit. Tommy's second foster family admitted him to the hospital. Mary says, "I was assigned to help Tommy. As a volunteer, I was in charge of feeding him and keeping track of his sleep and play periods. Then I was able to help find him a new foster family that could cope with his special needs."

A year later, they brought him back for a follow-up visit, and he had changed dramatically. "He brought me a photo of himself swimming in a lake," says Mary. "I realized that Tommy had finally learned how to trust. Tommy knew that his new foster family would not hurt or desert him. He was happy and secure for the first time in his life."

Questions to Ask Yourself

Human services work requires a great deal of dedication to the job. 1) Do you like to work independently or do you prefer to have more direction? 2) Are you a good listener? 3) Do you want to work in a hospital, or would you rather work on the streets?

National Service: Helping People in Your Country

4

Jobs in *national service* help people throughout the country. *National service workers* share their skills and experience to help people in disadvantaged communities. Programs such as Volunteers In Service To America (VISTA), Teach for America, and Habitat for Humanity send volunteers to work in the field. *In the field* means at a site, or the place where the work needs to be done. The volunteers live and work at a local level. They live in the same kind of conditions as the people they are helping.

Many of these programs have national offices called headquarters, where workers coordinate the programs. They provide support to the volunteers in the field. For instance, the workers at headquarters make sure that the volunteers have the supplies that they need, a monthly salary, and proper medical care. They also design and make goals for the programs. The directors of Habitat for

There are many national organizations that serve people in need. People who work for Habitat for Humanity build low-income houses.

Humanity choose the communities in which to build homes. The people in the VISTA office recruit volunteers from around the country.

Anne, College Student and Volunteer

Two weeks before spring break, Anne still had no plans for her future. With her week off from classes, she wanted to do something fun. She signed up for a program at college called "Spring Break in Appalachia." This program sponsors service projects in poor mountain communities. With a group of ten students, Anne drove from Washington, DC, to Grundy County, Tennessee.

The job there was to repair the Anderson family's one-room home. Anne rolled up her sleeves, picked up a hammer, and went to work. It was hard work peeling off old wallpaper, nailing beams, inserting insulation, and finally repaneling the walls. Anne slept well that week.

By seeing how other people live, Anne gained a new perspective on her own life. She learned that education involves more than books. Anne learned more from the Anderson family that week than she had from a whole semester of classes. Anne decided to incorporate helping people into her lifestyle.

You can help people in your community by working in a local homeless shelter or soup kitchen.

Americorps

Started by President Clinton in 1993, *Americorps* is a national service program that helps poor communities in America. Members work for one or two years. During this time they are given a living allowance to cover such expenses as food and housing. At the end of their service, they receive credit vouchers that can be traded in to pay for school. This money can help pay for college, graduate school, or other job training. The money can also be used to pay off existing student loans. Full-time workers receive $4,725 for serving 1,700 hours. Part-time workers receive $2,362.50 for 900 hours of service.

The Americorps program sends volunteers all over the country. The projects vary from education to public safety to the environment to human needs. To apply for a position with the Americorps program, you must be at least eighteen years old, a citizen or legal resident of the United States, and have a high school diploma or have passed the GED tests.

Volunteers In Service To America (VISTA)

The VISTA program is a full-time, year-long program open to men and women at least eighteen years old. VISTA volunteers serve in both urban and rural communities. Urban areas refer to the city, while rural refer to the country. The VISTA volunteers live and work in low-income communities. They live among the people that they help. By sharing their skills and experience, VISTA volunteers train local leaders in new methods. The volunteers teach in schools, develop environmental-protection projects, create community centers, and address public safety issues.

In return for their service, the volunteers receive educational awards and a small sum of

Another service you can provide is to teach people how to read.

money to cover basic living expenses, like food and travel. VISTA volunteers receive a monthly living allowance of $640. At the end of their service, they receive $4,725. They can use this money to help pay for their education, and they have up to seven years to use the award.

Other Domestic Programs

Teach for America sends teachers to inner-city schools that do not have enough teachers. Started by a college student named Wendy Kopp, the program recruits recent college graduates. The idea of the program is to get bright young college students interested in teaching. They bring new ideas and enthusiasm into some of the toughest classrooms in America. For one or two years, the new teachers gain valuable teaching experience. They also provide a needed service to these communities. The program is open to college graduates, and the application process is quite competitive.

Habitat for Humanity is an ecumenical housing ministry. Ecumenical means that the mission of the program is to promote unity among peoples. Workers build simple, affordable housing for people in need. The standard term of service is three years. The people in this program must be willing to work with people of diverse cultural and racial backgrounds. This work requires flexibility, patience, compassion, and a commitment to learn from the people you help. There is a six- to eight-week training course at the international headquarters. Workers earn a monthly stipend of $400 per month to cover basic living expenses.

Several states have *educational outreach programs*. One example of such a program is the *Mississippi Teacher Corps*, a volunteer program that sends teachers to poor communities in rural Mississippi. The term of service is one year. Teachers help promote good study habits and a broader understanding of the world beyond their students' immediate surroundings.

Executives for all of these programs work in offices and provide support for volunteers in the field. Executives design the programs. You can decide whether you want to work directly with people or behind the scenes in an office.

Questions to Ask Yourself

There are many options for people who want to help other communities in the United States. These are some things to consider when deciding which job you might like to pursue. 1) Do you like working in direct contact with people? 2) Are you willing to live in non-luxury surroundings? 3) Are you willing to relocate to another part of the country?

International Jobs: Helping People in the World

5

International jobs provide help to people in other countries. The variety of tasks is wide. For example, you can work in a relief organization. *Relief organizations* provide emergency services to people during disasters.

International jobs are not for everyone. The qualities that make a good worker in an overseas position are flexibility, cross-cultural sensitivity, and resourcefulness. Flexibility means being able to change and adapt readily to different situations. Flexible people are ready to accept alternatives if their plans do not work out. Having cross-cultural sensitivity means having respect for peoples from different countries. You accept local customs, behaviors, and languages. You try to learn from other people. Finally, you must be resourceful. This means that you must be able to find creative solutions for a problem. There is no book to tell you how to deal with every

Relief organizations help communities recover from war or natural disasters, such as hurricanes or earthquakes.

situation. But with patience and luck, you can make the best with what you have.

Kenley, Peace Corps Volunteer

Kenley works as a Peace Corps volunteer in Samarkand, Uzbekistan. Uzbekistan is a country in Europe, near Afghanistan. Kenley's job as a volunteer is to teach English in a local grade school. Kenley's challenge as a teacher is to make his English classes fun. But there are many challenges. The English textbooks that the school has provided Kenley are very old. Plus, the books are boring. There are no color illustrations, only tiny black-and-white sketches.

Kenley wrote to USAID (United States Agency for International Development) asking for money to buy books. USAID is an organization that funds projects in poor countries. Kenley was able to buy new books with color photos for the school. He brought his portable piano to school and taught lyrics from Whitney Houston's song "The Greatest Love of All" and the Beatles' "Let It Be." Suddenly the students started paying more attention in class. Most importantly, Kenley taught the other teachers to use his teaching methods. The local teachers began to use songs and games in their classes. The students want to study when their classes are fun. In this way, Kenley has made a lasting contribution in Uzbekistan. His presence will be felt as long as the Uzbek teachers continue to use his teaching methods.

The Peace Corps

On March 1, 1961, President John F. Kennedy issued an order creating the *Peace Corps*. Its mission was to promote world peace and friendship by providing qualified volunteers to interested countries. Today it sends an average of 6,000 U.S. citizens abroad each year.

Volunteers live at a local level in their host countries. They are paid in local currency. Each month they receive a small sum of money that covers basic living expenses, and varies with the local economy. For example, volunteers in Micronesia make the equivalent of $300 per month, while those in Turkmenistan make $75. Most volunteers live with host families. This is a great chance to learn the language and the culture.

For each month that they spend overseas, volunteers receive $200. At the end of their service, the volunteers receive a lump sum of about $5,000. This money helps them to get back on their feet in the United States.

As a Peace Corps volunteer, you will share your skills with people in the country in which you are placed. You will also learn new skills and ways of doing things.

Serving countries all over the world, the Peace Corps lives up to its promise as "the toughest job you'll ever love." Volunteers do everything from teaching English to sharing tips on growing food to providing preventive health care. However, the application process to become a Peace Corps volunteer is very competitive. You must be a U.S. citizen, at least eighteen years old, in good health, and willing to serve for two years. Nearly all volunteers have a bachelor's degree in their chosen field, and about 18 percent have their master's or doctorate degrees. Knowing a language, especially French or Spanish, helps.

The American Red Cross

Clara Barton founded the American Association of the Red Cross in 1881. Her organization was based on the Red Cross, founded by Jean-Henri Dunant, in Switzerland, nearly twenty years before. Now called *The American Red Cross*, it has become the largest humanitarian organization in the United States. *Humanitarian organizations* try to relieve pain and suffering in the world. The American Red Cross helps 30 million people a year to prevent, prepare for, and cope with

Humanitarian organizations often recruit volunteers from around the country to help a community faced with a disaster such as a flood.

such emergencies as hurricanes, floods, fires, earthquakes, and other natural disasters. The American Red Cross provides food, shelter, medicines, and clothing to victims of these disasters.

Many countries around the world have chapters of the Red Cross. These organizations belong to the International Red Cross. They each have the authority to enter disaster areas around the world. Since the International Red Cross is based in Switzerland, a politically neutral country, the organizations are considered politically neutral. They are allowed to work in troubled areas around the globe because of this neutrality.

The American Red Cross is divided into many departments, with a variety of jobs available in each section. The jobs range from volunteer to entry-level to professional to management. Call your local chapter to find out about the availability of jobs in your area. Keep in mind that volunteer experience with the Red Cross may help you get a paid position.

UNICEF

United Nations Children's Fund, also known as UNICEF, is an international organization working for children in 137 countries. Developed in 1946, it was originally called the United Nations International Children's Emergency Fund. UNICEF was the first organization devoted to the well-being of children around the world. It is now devoted to the needs of mothers and children in all developing countries. UNICEF provides relief and shelter to victims of natural disasters and war. It also evacuates children from areas facing these threats. UNICEF offers vaccines to those who don't have access to or can't afford medical services. It also helps people all over the world learn to read.

Questions to Ask Yourself
International jobs require a lot of resourcefulness. 1) Would you like to live in a foreign country? Why? 2) Would you rather work directly with people or behind the scenes? Would you rather teach others or help victims survive disasters? 3) Are you willing to learn another language and another culture? What language?

Finding the Right Job for You   6

Finding the right job is like solving a mystery. Certain things must happen before the mystery can be solved. The first of these things is knowing yourself well enough to select the best job for you. After that, there is research to do, a résumé to write, and an interview to pass. Let's take these one by one.

Know Yourself and What You Like

Reviewing the following questions may help you focus on your strengths, weaknesses, preferences, and dislikes. The answers will help you decide whether a career in the helping professions is really for you. They may also help you narrow down the choices within the field of the helping professions. Write your answers on a separate sheet of paper.

- Do you work well under pressure?
- Are you a good listener?
- Do you like to work with people on a one-

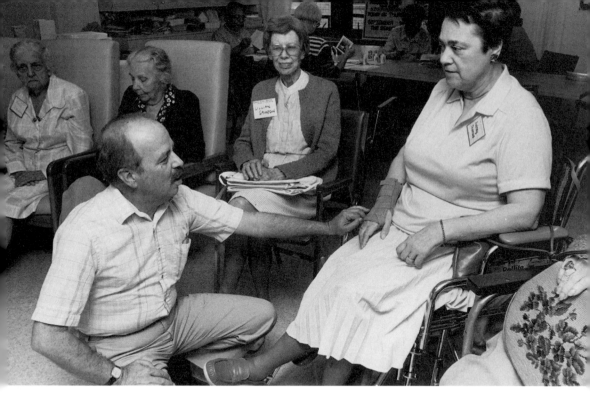

By knowing yourself and understanding what you like to do, you can narrow down your career search to jobs that really appeal to you.

to-one basis? Or do you prefer to work "behind the scenes," for instance by entering data in the computer or taking care of paperwork?
- How important is money to you? Will the amount of money you earn affect why you may like or dislike a job?
- What sort of atmosphere would you like to work in? Corporate? Informal? In a large office? A small office? Indoors? Outdoors?
- Is there a certain group of people you would like to work with? Infants, children, teenagers, adults, or the elderly? Or would you enjoy working with people in other countries, injured people, economically

disadvantaged people, or people who are looking for jobs?

Keeping your answers in mind, take another look at the careers mentioned in this book. You should have a much clearer idea of the kinds of careers that both appeal to you and that you have skills or qualities for. Now you're ready for the next step: learning more about that particular career.

Research

To begin the search for a specific job, you must do research. This means finding out more information. Most of the jobs in the helping professions are in both the public and private sectors of the workplace.

The *public sector* consists of jobs in government, in both federal and state agencies. These include national government organizations, such as the Peace Corps, and state social services, such as welfare. To get a government job, you must take a civil service test, which tests your general knowledge as well as the specifics of your career field. You can learn the dates and places of these tests by asking your guidance counselor or local librarian.

Jobs in the *private sector* are with private clinics, hospitals, businesses, or agencies that are not run by the government. These jobs are listed in the classified section of your local newspaper or in magazines or newspapers specific to your field.

Take a look at the classified section of your local newspaper under the headings of particular careers such as "medical field" or "counseling." Another way to find out about job listings is to look in the yellow pages of your telephone book under "helping services" or a similar heading. Call some of the numbers and ask whom you can speak with to find out whether they have any openings. If they do not, ask if they can refer you to somewhere that does. Keep a list of the places you've called. You may want to try them again in a couple of months.

Preparing a Résumé

A *résumé* is a written record of your education, experience, and accomplishments. There are many good books on writing résumés. Check out a couple from the library. Keep in mind that a résumé must be accurate, neat, and complete.

When you send your résumé out, include a

cover letter with it. A *cover letter* is a short letter of introduction. It explains how you heard about the job, why you are interested, and gives a brief explanation of why you think you are a good candidate. Remember that you are also enclosing your résumé, which gives your complete history. Your cover letter should also be accurate, containing absolutely no mistakes. The book on résumés should give you some tips about writing cover letters.

Interviews

Now that you have your list of job possibilities, people to contact, and a résumé, it is time to begin meeting some possible employers.

An *interview* is simply two people meeting to decide whether they suit each other's needs. The question the interviewer wants to answer is, "Will this person work well with our team?" The question you want to answer is, "How can I help this organization?"

In addition to two copies of your résumé, you should take your social security card, driver's license, and the name, phone numbers, and addresses of at least three references. *References* are people who know you who will give a good account of your personality, responsibility, and general abilities. Be sure to ask these people's permission before using them as references. You may also want to do some research on the place or position for which you are interviewing. This will help you figure out what questions to ask during the interview.

In general people dress conservatively for interviews. This means a jacket and tie for males, and a dress, skirt, or pantsuit for females. When you meet the interviewer, shake hands and use his or her name. Answer each question thoughtfully. Don't be afraid to take a little time to think about the question before you answer, but don't stall. Be honest with your answers. Ask questions about the position or company. The interviewer will raise the issue of salary and benefits when he or she is ready to offer you the job.

At the end of the interview, smile, thank the interviewer, and stand as you shake hands good-bye. It is essential that you follow up with a letter of thanks, restating your interest in the position and indicating that you look forward to hearing from the interviewer. The rest is up to the interviewer.

In the meantime, continue your

volunteering, networking, researching, and interviewing.

Final Decisions

It will take some time to decide on a career. You may change your mind once you volunteer or even after you get your first paid position in that field. That's okay. Try another area. No one says that you have to stick to one career for your entire life. The trick is not to be afraid to try something out. You may find that you love what you do. That is often the case for people who work in the helping professions. These people are everyday heroes. And you can be one too.

Questions to Ask Yourself

There are many steps to beginning a career. 1) What would be your first step in exploring a career that you're interested in? 2) If you want to start networking, who are the people you know who could help you? What would you talk to them about? 3) Where can you find out about job possibilities in your community?

Glossary

CPR (cardiopulmonary resuscitation) Emergency medical care to the victim of a heart attack.
CPT (cardiopulmonary technician) Person trained to administer CPR.
EMT (emergency medical technician) Life-support worker at the scene of an accident.
gerontology Study of the aging and their problems.
intern One who works for little or no pay in order to gain experience in the field.
networking Talking to people to exchange career information and job tips.
paraprofessional One who has received some education in a field.
private sector Businesses and other non-governmental organizations.
professional One who has received higher education in his or her field.
public sector Federal, state, and local government organizations.
relief organizations Groups that provide emergency services for people during times of disaster.
résumé Written record of a person's education, experience, and accomplishments.
salary Amount of money one is paid per year for doing a job.
volunteer One who works without pay.

For More Information

For information on government job opportunities, look for the numbers of these agencies in your local phone book.

- local offices of your state employment agency
- local offices of the United States Office of Personnel Management

The American Red Cross
National Headquarters
8111 Gatehouse Road
Falls Church, VA 22042
(703) 206-6000
http://www.crossnet.org/jobs/index.html

Americorps and Volunteers In Service to America (VISTA) are both located in the same headquarters:
1201 New York Avenue, NW
Washington, DC 20525
(800) 942-2677

Habitat for Humanity
121 Habitat Street
Americus, GA 31709
(912) 924-6935

National Association of Rehabilitation
　Agencies
11250 Roger Bacon Drive
Reston, VA 22090
(703) 437-4377

National Organization for Human Services
　Education
Brookdale Community College
Lyncroft, NJ 07738
(908) 224-2000

Peace Corps
1990 K Street, NW
Washington, DC 20526
(800) 424-8580
http://www.clark.net/pub/peace/
PeaceCorps.html

Division of Information
UNICEF
3 UN Plaza
New York, NY 10017
(212) 326-7000

For Further Reading

Abbott, Marguerite. *Opportunities in Occupational Therapy Careers*. Lincolnwood, IL: VGM Career Horizons, 1995.

Barber, James. *Social Work with Addictions*. New York: New York University Press, 1994.

Bernstein, Gail S. *"Human Services? That Must Be So Rewarding."* Baltimore: Brooks Publishing Company, 1989.

Brearly, Judith. *Counseling and Social Work*. Bristol, PA: Open University Press, 1995.

Faux, Marian. *The Complete Resume Guide*. New York: Prentice Hall, 1992.

Paradis, Lex. *Careers for Caring People*. Lincolnwood, IL: VGM Career Horizons, 1995.

Wilkinson, Beth. *Careers Inside the World of Health Care*. New York: Rosen Publishing Group, 1995.

Williams, Ellen. *Gerontology and Aging Services*. Lincolnwood, IL: VGM Career Horizons, 1995.

Yates, Martin John. *Cover Letters That Knock 'em Dead*. Holbrook, MA: Bob Adams, 1992.

Index

A
aide/assistant, 11–12, 32, 33
alcohol and drug abuse counselor, 32
American Red Cross, 16, 48–50
Americorps, 38–39
apprenticeship, 10–11
associate, 13

C
candy stripers, 14
case work, 28
certification, 21, 33
　board, 26
　state, 12-13, 16, 17, 21
child abuse counselors, 32
child welfare workers, 30
civil service test, 54–55
community outreach workers, 32
community organization work, 29
counseling, 27, 28–29
cover letter, 56

E
education, 22, 33
　college, 12, 13, 17, 26, 31, 48
educational outreach programs, 41
Emergency Medical Services, 19
emergency medical technician (EMT), 19–22
entry-level jobs, 10, 11–12, 50
executives, 42

G
gerontology counselors, 32
gerontology social workers, 31
group work, 28–29

H
Habitat for Humanity, 35–37, 41
health care, 9
　home, 22–23
　workers, 14
helping professions, 9–13
　finding a job in, 52–58
human services, 9, 27–34
humanitarian organizations, 48

I
industrial social workers, 30–31
intern, 10–11
International Red Cross, 49–50
international service, 9
interview, 52, 56–58

M
medical assistants, 24
medical social workers, 30
Mississippi Teacher Corps, 41–42

N
national service, 9, 35
networking, 11, 58
nurse's aide, 14–17
nursing homes, 16

O
occupational social workers, 30–31

P
paramedic, 19, 20, 21, 22
paraprofessional jobs, 10, 12–13

63

Peace Corps, 45–48, 54
personal care facility, 14, 16
physical therapist, 17–18
   aide, 18
   assistant, 17
physician, 24–26
private sector, 55
professional, 13
public sector, 54

R
references, 56
relief organizations, 43
résumé, 52, 55–56

S
school social workers, 30
social workers, 27, 29–32

T
Teach for America, 35, 40–41

U
United Nations Children's Fund (UNICEF), 50–51
United States Agency for International Development (USAID), 45

V
vocational rehabilitation counselors, 32
Volunteers In Service To America (VISTA), 35, 37, 39–40
volunteer jobs, 10–11, 33–34, 37–42, 45–48, 50, 58

Contributing Editor: Beatrice Grabish

About the Author
A former English teacher, Pat Tretout has also worked in the publishing industry. She is currently involved in several free-lance projects. Ms. Tretout's work has been published in several publications, including *The New York Times*.

Photo Credits: Cover © Janeart/Image Bank; pp. 2, 6, 15 © Skjold Photographs; p. 8 © Patrick Ramsey/International Stock; p. 10 © Meryl Levin/Impact Visuals; p. 12 © Ansel Horn/Impact Visuals; p. 18, 31 © AP/Wide World Photos; p. 21© Tom McKitterick/Impact Visuals; p. 23 © Barros & Barros/Image Bank; p. 25 © David W. Hamilton/Image Bank; pp. 36, 47 © Jim West/Impact Visuals; p. 38 © Scott Thode/International Stock; p. 40 © Donna Binder/Impact Visuals; p. 44 © Ryan Williams/International Stock; p. 49 © Jeff Scott/Impact Visuals; p. 53 © Martha Tabor/Impact Visuals.

Book Design: Erin McKenna